MW01064251

DESTINATION
MARS

GILES SPARROW

PowerKiDS
press
New York

Published in 2010 by The Rosen Publishing Group
29 East 21st Street, New York, NY 10010

© 2010 The Brown Reference Group Ltd

All rights reserved. No part of this book may be reproduced in any form
without permission in writing from the publisher, except by a reviewer.

U.S. Editor: Kara Murray

Picture Credits
Key: t – top, b – below, c – center, l – left, r – right. Daein Ballard: 29l;
ESA: DLR 12t, 12b, MPS TP, 2, 7; NASA: 13, 23l, 25b, GSFC 15, JPL 8-9,
9b, 10-11, 11c, 14-15, 20l, 26, 28b, JPL/Corby Waste 24t, JSC 6-7, LaRC
21t, 24b, SAIC/Pat Rawlings 29r; Photos.com: 21b; Science Photo Library:
NASA 23r, 25c, 28t, Omikron 20bc, Detlev Van Ravenswaay 9c, 18, 22,
27, Steve Munsinger 19; Shutterstock: Spectral-Design 2-3, 16-17,
George Toubalis 4t, 4b

Front cover: NASA: bl; ESA: MPS c; Back cover: ESA: MPS; Backgrounds:
NASA

Special thanks to Science Photo Library

Library of Congress Cataloging-in-Publication Data

Sparrow, Giles.
  Destination Mars / Giles Sparrow. — 1st ed.
     p. cm. — (Destination solar system)
  Includes index.
  ISBN 978-1-4358-3443-9 (lib. bdg.) — ISBN 978-1-4358-3459-0 (pbk.)
  — ISBN 978-1-4358-3460-6 (6-pack)
  1. Mars (Planet)—Juvenile literature. 2. Mars probes—Juvenile
literature. I. Title.
  QB641.S6739 2010
  523.43—dc22

                                          2008055102

Manufactured in China

CONTENTS

WHERE IS MARS?

Mars is our next-door neighbor. It is the fourth planet from the Sun, Earth is the third. Mars is smaller than Earth but being so close, it is often easy to see. It looks like an orange star in the night's sky.

Mars goes around the Sun in a circle called an **orbit**. The time it takes a planet to go around the Sun once is its year. The Martian year is 687 Earth days, nearly twice as long as our own year.

Imagine you are about to set off on a **mission** to Mars. How long will it take to get there? Mars is usually about 141 million miles (227 million km) from the Sun.

SIZE COMPARED TO EARTH

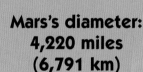

**Mars's diameter:
4,220 miles
(6,791 km)**

**Earth's diameter:
7,926 miles
(12,756 km)**

DISTANCE FROM THE SUN

Mars is the fourth of the four rocky planets, which are closest to the Sun. The next four planets are made from clouds of gas or balls of ice. The dwarf planet Pluto is made from ice.

Sun Mercury Venus Earth Mars Jupiter Saturn

0   500 (805)   1,000 (1,609)

Distance in millions of miles (millions of km)

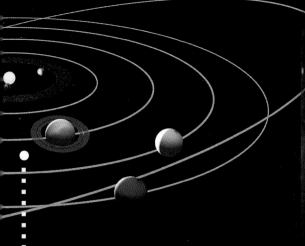

The solar system is made up of the Sun, the planets, and the asteroid belt—a ring of rocks that orbit between Mars and Jupiter.

However, the distance between Earth and Mars varies a lot. When the two planets are on the same side of the Sun, it takes about six months to fly there. When Mars is on the opposite side of the Sun to us, the journey takes closer to five years!

Your journey will begin when Mars is nearest to us. The planet is in this position for just a few months every few years. You must be ready to leave on time.

Getting to Mars

The time it takes to reach Mars depends on how you travel, and on the positions of Mars and Earth in their orbits when you set off.

Distance from Earth to Mars
Closest	35 million miles (56 million km)
Farthest	248 million miles (400 million km)

By car at 70 miles per hour (113 km/h)
Closest	57 years
Farthest	404 years

By rocket at 7 miles per second (11 km/s)
Closest	58 days
Farthest	410 days

Time for radio signals to reach Mars (at the speed of light)
Closest	3 minutes 8 seconds
Farthest	22 minutes 13 seconds

Uranus

Neptune

Pluto

2,000 (3,219)   2,500 (4,023)   3,000 (4,828)   3,500 (5,633)

FIRST VIEW

Your journey begins with a short rocket flight into orbit to meet up with your giant spacecraft. You will spend months flying through space but have only a few days on Mars.

THE RED PLANET

Mars is small compared to Earth, and you need to get close before you can see the planet clearly. On your final approach, you get a breathtaking view. Much of the planet is red with dark brown patches. However, the **poles** appear to be white, as if covered in ice.

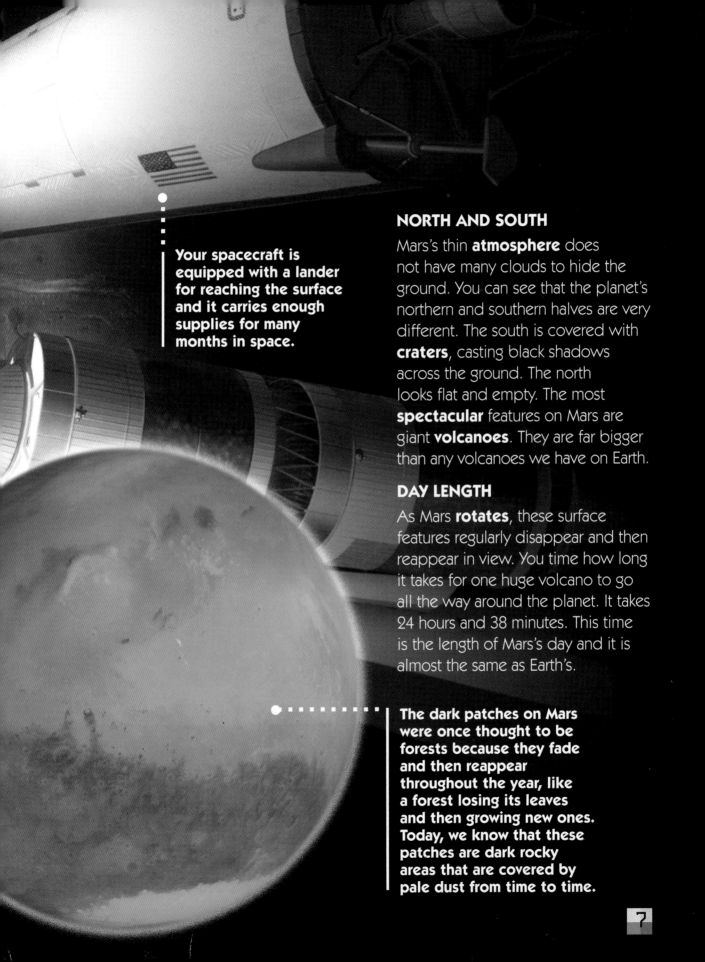

Your spacecraft is
equipped with a lander
for reaching the surface
and it carries enough
supplies for many
months in space.

NORTH AND SOUTH

Mars's thin **atmosphere** does
not have many clouds to hide the
ground. You can see that the planet's
northern and southern halves are very
different. The south is covered with
craters, casting black shadows
across the ground. The north
looks flat and empty. The most
spectacular features on Mars are
giant **volcanoes**. They are far bigger
than any volcanoes we have on Earth.

DAY LENGTH

As Mars **rotates**, these surface
features regularly disappear and then
reappear in view. You time how long
it takes for one huge volcano to go
all the way around the planet. It takes
24 hours and 38 minutes. This time
is the length of Mars's day and it is
almost the same as Earth's.

The dark patches on Mars
were once thought to be
forests because they fade
and then reappear
throughout the year, like
a forest losing its leaves
and then growing new ones.
Today, we know that these
patches are dark rocky
areas that are covered by
pale dust from time to time.

ON THE SURFACE

As your lander touches down, it throws up a cloud of dust, blocking the view through the windows. You wait for the dust to clear before putting on your spacesuit and opening the door for a look outside.

A DESERT PLANET

At first Mars looks like a rocky desert on Earth. Then you notice something strange—the sky is pink! The rocks are reddish orange. This color comes from iron oxide in the rock. This is the same chemical in rusty iron.

The **gravity** on Mars is only a third of Earth's, so your body weighs a lot less.

Mars's polar ice caps grow in winter and get smaller in summer. This image shows an ice age on Mars when ice covered half the planet.

DRY ICE SHEET

In the distance you see a white hill. It is the edge of the thin **ice cap** covering the north pole of Mars. There is another in the south. Mars's polar ice caps are very different from Earth's. The ice is mostly frozen **carbon dioxide**, the main gas in Mars's air. Only the north pole has some water ice, as Earth's ice caps have.

Frozen carbon dioxide is known as dry ice. It does not melt into a liquid. Instead it forms a smoky gas. When Mars's ice caps melt in summer, they do not form any liquids. Mars is dry all year.

WHIRLWINDS

Visitors to Mars would need to watch out for ferocious whirlwinds that sweep across the planet like tornadoes (below). They are caused by swirling winds that suck dust up from the ground. Each whirlwind produces a looping trail of clouds above the surface of Mars. These plumes can been seen from orbit.

Mars looks like a desert. The sky even looks pink because dust is blown into the air by the wind.

MARTIAN
LANDSCAPE

Northern Mars is flat, while the south is covered in rocky hills. Between the two there is a huge bump in the surface, called the Tharsis Bulge. You decide to take a flying tour of this spectacular region of Mars.

BIG LUMP

The Tharsis Bulge runs along Mars's **equator** and covers about a quarter of the planet. **Astronomers** think it is formed by **magma** pushing up from inside the planet, making volcanoes. Huge canyons form where the ground splits as the bulge is pushed up.

SUPERGRAND CANYON

The biggest canyon on Mars is the Valles Marineris. This is a vast, steep-sided canyon that runs for 2,500 miles (4,000 km) along Mars's equator. The Valles Marineris is 10 times longer and 4 times deeper than Earth's Grand Canyon. In fact, it is almost big enough to swallow the entire Himalayas. Only the tallest peaks would poke out above the rim!

The Valles Marineris is the largest canyon in the solar system. It would reach across the United States completely.

CRATER FACE

Most of Mars's impact craters are in the south. By far the largest is the Hellas Basin, which is 1,400 miles (2,250 km) wide. It was made by a huge impact about 4 billion years ago. Older craters on Mars have been slowly worn away by wind and landslides.

GIANT MOUNTAINS

Four huge volcanoes stick out of the Tharsis Bulge. The most spectacular is Olympus Mons, which rises 17 miles (27 km) above the surface. Olympus Mons is the tallest mountain in the whole **solar system**.

The Martian volcanoes ooze **lava** slowly over millions of years, building up layer after layer with each **eruption**. As the lava piles up, the center of the volcano caves in and forms a sunken crater.

Today the volcanoes on Mars are silent. Astronomers think they have been dormant for 150 million years. However, the monster volcanoes might explode into action again one day.

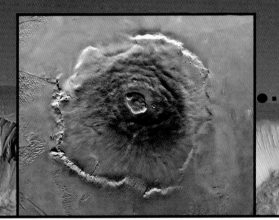

The crater of Olympus Mons is 56 miles (90 km) wide.

Olympus Mons —————————— Everest

Olympus Mons is three times taller than Mount Everest, but it is so wide that you would hardly notice the slope if you climbed it.

WATER WORLD

Astronomers have found what look like river valleys on Mars (below). They were probably made by flowing water billions of years ago. Scientists think that there was once enough water on Mars to cover the whole planet to a depth of about 1,640 feet (500 m).

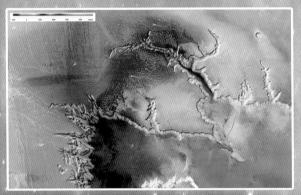

ANCIENT OCEANS

Astronomers think that Mars once had much more water than it does today. Most of it would have collected in the northern plains, which are the lowest part of the surface. The plains have broad canyons and **gullies** that seem to have formed in powerful floods. Other areas have winding valleys that were worn away by rivers.

DISAPPEARING WATER

One of the biggest mysteries about Mars is where all its water went. There is some proof that water sometimes flows on Mars even today. For example, some Martian craters have small gullies in their rims, where water appears to have briefly flowed downhill, perhaps after seeping out from under ground.

Mars has landscape features that must have been made by erosion by liquid water.

WHAT'S THE WEATHER LIKE?

The Sun is up over Mars for the same amount of time each day as it is on Earth. However, Mars is a freezing desert, with dry and bitterly cold weather.

MISTY DAWN ON MARS

You decide to spend a whole day on Mars, so you land your ship on the dark side of the planet just before dawn. Outside, the nighttime **temperature** is a chilly −193°F (−125°C) and a layer of frost covers the ground.

As the Sun rises, the temperature slowly rises to about freezing. As the first rays of sunlight hit the ground, the frost **evaporates**, but it then **condenses** in the cold air, forming a blanket of mist.

WEAK WIND

Soon the mist has gone, and the wind has picked up, whipping up clouds of fine dust. However, Mars's air is so thin that you feel no effects of even fast winds.

SNOW CLOUDS

It snows high in Mars's atmosphere, although as far as we know it does not reach the ground. Snowflakes form in clouds about 2.5 miles (4 km) above the poles.

MARTIAN SEASONS

Like Earth, Mars spins on a tilted axis, and this causes seasons. When the north pole is tilted toward the Sun, it is summer in the north and winter in the south. When the south pole is tilted toward the Sun, it is summer in the south and winter in the north. Mars's year is almost twice as long as an Earth year, so seasons on Mars last much longer, and the weather gets more extreme.

SUNSHINE AND CLOUDS

By midday the temperature is still quite chilly. Mars's thin atmosphere cannot trap much of the Sun's heat. Even on the hottest days on Mars, it rarely gets much above 68°F (20°C).

The pink sky is clear most of the time, but sometimes small white clouds appear. These are most common around the poles in winter or near the equator in summer.

Mars's air is too cold for its clouds to have liquid water in them. Instead the clouds are made of crystals of water ice and frozen carbon dioxide. They are always thin and wispy.

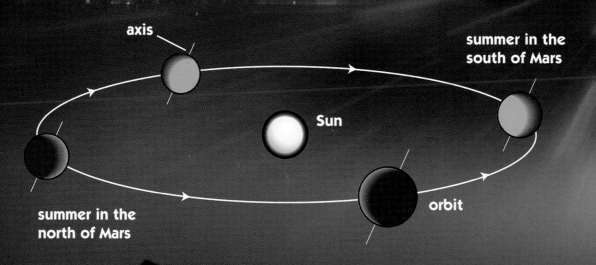

axis

summer in the south of Mars

Sun

summer in the north of Mars

orbit

DARK BLUE SUNSET

In the evening, more hazy clouds start to form as the air begins to cool. As the Sun sinks low on the horizon, the sky changes color in a beautiful sunset. However, unlike the fiery sunsets on Earth, the evening sky on Mars is dark blue! The air **filters** out any red light.

The surface features on Mars (left) are often hidden by immense dust storms that cover the whole planet for weeks on end (below).

Sunsets on Mars are blue not red!

HOW DID MARS FORM?

Mars formed 4.5 **billion** years ago from a cloud of gas and dust that surrounded a newly born star—the Sun.

BALLS OF DUST

Dust in the cloud began to stick together into larger clumps. **Eventually** one clump grew big enough to draw in all the others nearby with its pull of gravity. They formed large lumps, or **planetesimals**.

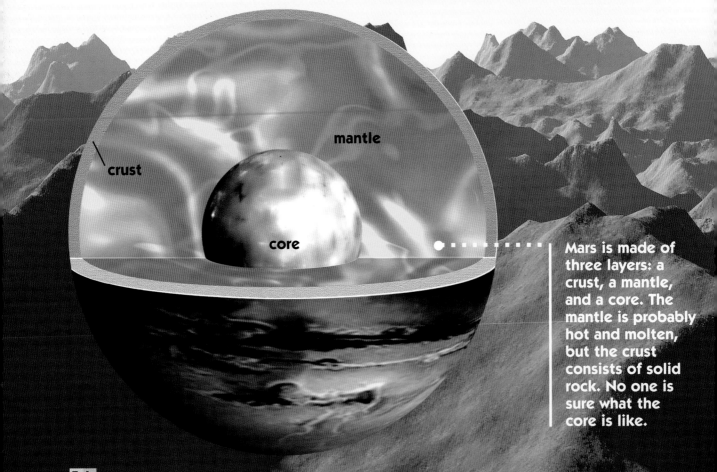

crust

mantle

core

Mars is made of three layers: a crust, a mantle, and a core. The mantle is probably hot and molten, but the crust consists of solid rock. No one is sure what the core is like.

SMASHING TIME

The planetesimals smashed into each other, breaking apart or sticking together. With each **impact**, the growing planetesimals became hotter.

The heat melted the young planets. Heavy metals sank to the center, while lighter **minerals** rose to the surface. Mars ended up with an iron **core**, surrounded by a **mantle** of **semimolten** rock and topped by a solid **crust**, just like Earth.

FROZEN CORE?

Astronomers do not know how big Mars's core is or whether it is molten like Earth's or solid metal. One clue comes from the fact that Mars has no magnetic field. Earth's strong magnetism is caused by hot iron spinning in the core as the planet rotates. Perhaps the reason that Mars has no magnetism is because its core is frozen solid.

STUCK SOLID

On Earth, the solid crust split into huge slabs, called plates. These drift slowly across Earth's surface, bumping into each other and forming mountain ranges and other features. The crust on Mars never formed plates, so its surface has not moved for a very long time.

Without plates, Mars's crust has stayed in the same place for millions of years. Its volcanoes are so huge because they have been erupting and growing in the same place for billions of years.

BLOWN AWAY

Astronomers think that long ago Mars was covered by a much thicker atmosphere. For some reason, it then lost most of its air. Perhaps the air was blasted off the planet by a huge impact with asteroids. After losing most of its atmosphere, Mars grew cold, and its water disappeared.

BIG HITTER

Astronomers have discovered that Mars has a thicker, lumpier crust under the southern highlands than beneath the northern plains. They think this is because the southern crust cooled quickly before it had time to flatten out. The northern plains stayed molten longer and so became smoother. This might have been caused by a large planetesimal hitting the northern half of Mars. That would have produced a lot of heat and melted the surface flat.

An artist's impression of the enormous impact when the planet was still cooling down that might have created Mars's smooth northern plains.

© D. van Ravenswaay

MOONS OF MARS

Before heading home you decide to visit Mars's two tiny moons, Phobos and Deimos.

Mars's ice cap is clear to see from the surface of Deimos, it smaller moon. The moon's name means "panic" in Greek.

LITTLE MOONS

Deimos is just 9 miles (14 km) wide. It orbits Mars once every 30 hours, traveling 12,400 miles (20,000 km) above the planet's surface. Earth's moon is 234,900 miles (378,000 km) up.

Phobos is larger but even closer to Mars. It is 17 miles (27 km) wide and orbits 3,700 miles (6,000 km) high. Being so near to the ground means it needs to move fast to stay in orbit. Phobos takes just 7 hours, 40 minutes to travel around Mars. However, Phobos is gradually getting closer to Mars. Eventually it will smash into the planet and be destroyed.

The name Phobos means "fear" in Greek. This moon has a 6-mile (10 km) crater named Stickney, for Asaph Hall's wife.

TRAPPED ASTEROIDS

When the Viking space **probes** visited Mars in the 1970s, scientists discovered that its moons are very different from other moons in the solar system. They are too small to have a regular shape, and both of them have a dark surface coated in minerals. These features suggest that the moons are really **asteroids** that were captured by Mars's gravity early in the planet's history.

FAILED MISSION

In 1988, the **Soviet Union** sent two probes to Phobos to solve the mysteries of Mars's moons. The probes carried landers to drop onto the moon to **analyze** the rocks. Sadly, both spacecraft broke down on the long journey to Mars.

MOON HUNTER

Phobos and Deimos were discovered by the American Asaph Hall in 1877. He saw that Mars wobbled as it orbited the Sun. He knew the planet was being affected by at least one moon. Eventually Hall found two, but they were much smaller and closer to Mars than expected.

EARLY DISCOVERIES

People have known about Mars since ancient times. The red planet was associated with war—Mars was the Roman war god. However, little was known about Mars until people looked at it with telescopes in the 1600s.

LIGHT AND DARK PATCHES

The first person to record **details** on Mars was the Dutch astronomer Christiaan Huygens, who saw a dark triangle on the planet in 1659. Huygens was also the first to notice the planet's pale ice caps.

CANAL CONFUSION

In 1877, the Italian astronomer Giovanni Schiaparelli published the first detailed map of the surface of Mars. This map caused a lot of trouble.

In the 1780s, astronomer William Herschel saw that stars did not grow dim as they passed close to Mars. He suggested that Mars's atmosphere was too thin to block out the starlight.

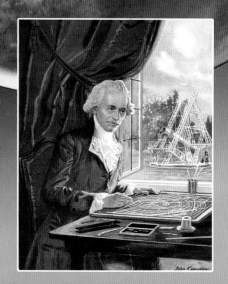

John Cameron

MARTIAN CIVILIZATION

Schiaparelli drew lines between the dark zones on the map. He thought the lines were rivers. He labeled them *canali*, the Italian word for "channels." However, other people thought he had seen canals, or waterways that had been dug by **aliens**. Many people believed that Mars was home to an alien civilization. The truth was only revealed when space probes sent back pictures of a desert planet.

Shiaparelli's map of Mars showed a network of channels, which people thought had been made by aliens.

Percival Lowell was a rich American businessman and astronomer. He became so obsessed with finding canals on Mars that he built an observatory in Flagstaff, Arizona, to search for signs of life on the red planet. He found nothing. However, Pluto was discovered in 1930 using Lowell's telescope.

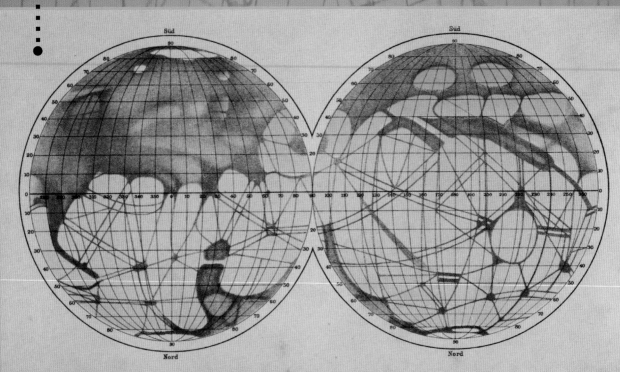

Die Verdoppelungen der dunkeln Linien auf dem Planeten Mars.

EXPLORING MARS

Mariner 4 lifted off in November 1964 and reached Mars in July 1965. It did not orbit the planet but flew straight past.

W e have sent more space probes to Mars than to any other planet. Mars is the planet most like Earth and might be a place where people could live one day.

STAR SAILORS

The first probe to reach Mars was **NASA**'s *Mariner 4*. The probe gave astronomers their first good look at the planet. It also found that the planet did not have a strong **magnetic field**. Four years later, *Mariner 6* and *Mariner 7* arrived at Mars. The probes analyzed chemicals in the atmosphere and ice caps and took close-up photographs of the surface.

Mariner 4 was powered by four solar panels. It carried a camera and a dish to beam pictures to Earth.

DOWN TO THE SURFACE

Many people were disappointed that the Mariner missions showed Mars was a dead world more like the Moon than Earth. However, there was a lot more to discover. The next thing to do was get a robot probe to land on Mars. The Soviet Union sent two in 1971. One crash-landed, the other stopped working after 20 seconds.

NASA's two Viking landers touched down in 1976, sending back pictures of a rocky landscape and pink skies. The landers also had weather instruments and a robot arm to collected dirt for testing on board.

NEW ARRIVALS

The next probe to land on Mars was NASA's *Mars Pathfinder*, which arrived in July 1997. The lander carried *Sojourner*, the first remote-controlled **rover** to explore the surface of Mars. Shortly afterward, *Mars Global Surveyor* went into orbit and began to make a photographic record of the entire planet.

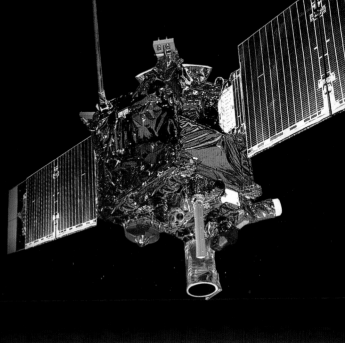

Mars Global Surveyor's cameras saw whirlwinds and landslides. Wobbles in its orbit were also used to pick up changes in Mars's gravity. That was used to measure the thickness of the planet's crust.

Astronomers thought that Mars had a blue sky, so that is the color they used in the first Viking pictures. But that made the rocks look green! Once the colors were corrected, they saw that the sky was actually pink.

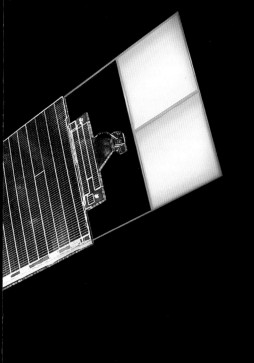

Space probes have not sent rocks back from Mars, but little bits of the planet have made it to Earth. These rocks were blasted into space when an asteroid hit Mars. They then landed on Earth as meteorites. One lump of Martian rock was found in Antarctica in 1984. In 1996, NASA scientists announced that this rock had structures that looked like bacteria (below) in it. However, scientists now think these are just mineral patterns.

The *Sojourner* rover spent three months rolling around the landing site. It had chemical sniffers to analyze rocks and 3-D cameras.

CURSE OF MARS

Many Mars probes do not make it. In 1999, *Climate Orbiter* and *Polar Lander* both failed. *Climate Orbiter* was lost because its controllers got mixed up between kilometers and miles! *Beagle 2* crashed on Mars in 2003 because the atmosphere was too thin for its parachute.

MORE ROVERS

After the success of *Sojourner*, NASA sent two more rovers in 2004. *Sojourner* was not much larger than a skateboard and weighed about the same as a dog. The next two rovers, *Spirit* and *Opportunity*, were 20 times heavier and almost as tall as a person. NASA plans to send an even larger rover, the *Mars Science Laboratory*, in 2010. This will be the size of a small car!

DOUBLE TEAM

Spirit and *Opportunity* arrived on Mars within days of each other. Both are powered by solar panels on their flat upper surfaces.

Spirit has six metal wheels fitted to a jointed suspension. The rover can roll straight over rocks in its way.

Both rovers carry the equipment for studying the rocks on Mars. They also have shovels and drills for digging into the surface. The rovers are also equipped with several cameras. They include a stereo camera, which scans the landscape like a pair of eyes to make detailed pictures. The rovers have been a huge success and are still exploring Mars today.

BOUNCEDOWN ON MARS

Spirit and *Opportunity* made unusual landings. Each probe plunged through the atmosphere protected by a heat shield. Then a parachute was released to slow the fall. A set of airbags filled with gas to protect the probe before it hit the ground. The bags bounced many times before rolling to a stop. Finally, the airbags deflated and solar panels folded open to power up the rover.

Even with its parachute, *Opportunity* hit the surface of Mars at more than 60 miles per hour (100 km/h) and rolled for 3,000 feet (900 m).

SEARCH FOR WATER

In 2004, NASA began to plan Project Constellation, a mission to send a crew of astronauts back to the Moon in 2020. The same spacecraft could be used to fly to Mars by 2050.

Constellation astronauts would have to spend several months on the surface of Mars and a supply of water in the planet's rocks would be very useful. It could be used to make **oxygen** and even turned into fuel to power the flight home.

PHOENIX LANDER

In the summer of 2008, the *Phoenix* spacecraft landed at Mars's north pole. Its mission was to dig into the frozen ground to find water ice. Scientists also hope to find signs of life there.

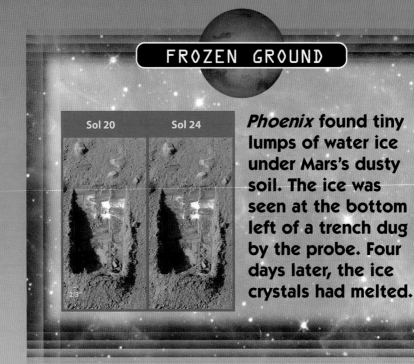

FROZEN GROUND

Sol 20   Sol 24

Phoenix found tiny lumps of water ice under Mars's dusty soil. The ice was seen at the bottom left of a trench dug by the probe. Four days later, the ice crystals had melted.

The *Phoenix* lander used braking rockets to make a soft landing on Mars.

COULD HUMANS LIVE THERE?

O f all the planets in the solar system besides Earth, Mars is the one where humans could live most easily.

MOVING TO MARS

Pumping gases into Mars's atmosphere will make the air thicker. The planet will get warmer and ice will melt. Plants could grow in the wet soil and produce oxygen. After many centuries, humans might be able to walk on Mars without spacesuits!

LONG STAY

Although it is most like Earth, walking without a spacesuit on Mars would kill you in seconds. The low **air pressure** would turn your blood into foam!

However, many countries are planning to send people to Mars by 2050. Crews would have to live on Mars for many months until Earth was close enough for the return journey.

Human explorers could discover much more about Mars than robot probes.

GLOSSARY

air pressure (EHR PREH-shur) A measure of how much the air pushes down on you. The air pressure on Mars is less than 1 percent of what it is on Earth.

aliens (AY-lee-unz) Creatures from outer space.

analyze (A-nuh-lyz) To find out about something using scientific tests.

asteroids (AS-teh-roydz) Large chunks of rock left over from when the planets formed.

astronomers (uh-STRAH-nuh-merz) Scientists who study planets and other objects in space.

atmosphere (AT-muh-sfeer) The layer of gas trapped around the surface of a planet.

billion (BIL-yun) A thousand millions.

carbon dioxide (KAR-bin dy-OK-syd) A heavy colorless gas. Carbon dioxide is found in the atmospheres of Earth, Venus, and Mars.

condenses (kun-DENTS-ez) Cools and changes from a gas to a liquid.

core (KOR) The central part of a planet.

craters (KRAY-turz) Holes made in the ground when a space rock smashes into a planet or moon. Volcanoes also produce a type of crater.

crust (KRUST) The solid outer surface of a planet or moon.

details (DEE-taylz) Extra facts.

equator (ih-KWAY-tur) An imaginary line around the center of a planet, moon, or star that is located midway between the poles.

eruption (ih-RUP-shun) When lava oozes out of a crack in the ground or the crater of a volcano.

evaporates (ih-VA-puh-rayts) When a liquid, such as water, boils into a gas, such as steam.

eventually (ih-VEN-chuh-wel-ee) At some point.

filters (FIL-turz) Takes something out of something else.

gravity (GRA-vih-tee) The force that pulls objects together. The heavier or closer an object is, the stronger its gravity.

gullies (GUH-leez) Narrow ditches made by flowing water.

ice cap (EYES KAP) A thick layer of ice that covers the ground. Most planets' ice caps are at the poles.

impact (IM-pakt) When two objects hit each other.

lava (LAH-vuh) Melted rock that pours onto a planet's surface.

magma (MAG-muh) A molten mixture of minerals that churns around inside a planet.

magnetic field (mag-NEH-tik FEELD) A region of space around a planet, moon, or star where a compass can detect the north pole.

mantle (MAN-tul) The section of a planet between the core and the crust.

minerals (MIN-rulz) Naturally occurring matter.

mission (MIH-shun) An expedition to visit a certain place in space, such as a planet.

NASA (NA-suh) The National Aeronautics and Space Administration, the U.S. space agency in charge of sending people and probes into space.

orbit (OR-bit) A movement around a heavier, and usually larger, object caused by the effect of the heavier object's gravity.

oxygen (OK-sih-jen) The invisible gas in Earth's air that living things breathe in.

planetesimals (pla-neh-TEH-suh-mulz) Small, planetlike balls that formed in the early solar system.

poles (POHLZ) The top or bottom end of the axis of a planet, moon, or star.

probes (PROHBZ) Robot spaceships sent to study the solar system.

rotates (ROH-tayts) Spins around a central point, or axis.

rover (ROH-vur) A remote-controlled wheeled vehicle sent to explore a moon or planet.

semimolten (seh-mee-MOHL-ten) Partly hot and liquid.

solar system (SOH-ler SIS-tem) The planets, asteroids, and comets that orbit the Sun.

Soviet Union (SOH-vee-et YOON-yun) An empire centered on Russia that ruled a huge area, stretching from Europe to East Asia, in the twentieth century.

spectacular (spek-TAK-yoo-lur) Very unusual and great.

temperature (TEM-pur-cher) How hot something is.

volcanoes (vol-KAY-nohz) Mountains formed from lava that erupts onto the surface from under ground.

INDEX

WEB SITES

Due to the changing nature of Internet links, PowerKids Press has developed an online list of Web sites related to the subject of this book. This site is updated regularly. Please use this link to access the list:
www.powerkidslinks.com/dsol/mars/

VESTAVIA HILLS PUBLIC LIBRARY
1112 MONTGOMERY HWY.
VESTAVIA HILLS, AL 35216
205-978-0155